KILL THE BLACK PARROT

Kill
the Black
Parrot

Dorothy Nimmo

LITTLEWOOD ARC
1993

Published by Littlewood Arc
Nanholme Mill, Shaw Wood Road
Todmorden, Lancs. OL14 6DA

Printed by Arc & Throstle Press Ltd
Nanholme Mill, Todmorden, Lancs.
Typeset by Lasertext, Stretford.

ISBN 0 946407 73 8

Acknowledgements are due to the
following magazines where
some of the poems have appeared:
*Writing Women, Rialto, Smiths Knoll,
Greenbook* and *Aquarius.*

Some poems from this collection
gained prizes at Bridport, Cardiff,
South Manchester and the
Prema Arts Centre.

The publishers acknowledge financial
assistance from Yorkshire and Humberside
Arts Board, North West Arts Board and
Arts Board South West.

CONTENTS

About the Author

BLACK PARROT

Kill the black parrot. Choke the sodding bird,
it never said a kind thing or a true word
or if it did that wasn't what I heard.

I only heard it squawking in my ear
things no-one in their right mind wants to hear
that made me cold with shame and white with fear.

Behave yourself. Control yourself. You know
you don't think that, you only think you do.
You can't just please yourself. I told you so.

You're being selfish. It's for your own good.
You must. You must not. But you know you should.
If you tried harder I am sure you could.

I'm disappointed in you. Never say
I didn't tell you. But you had your way,
you'd not be told. There'll be a price to pay.

Where was it Polly learned that canting word?
It's time to wring its neck, the stupid bird.

What made us think that was the voice of God?

BITCH

If I called her by her right name I could make her answer
my call.
If I knew her right name I could make her mind me,
I could make her mine, I could bend her to my will,
I could make her move or stop moving and be still.

I call her honey, her smile is sweet as I kiss it away.
I call her angel, gold leaf haloes her head.
I call her bird, she flicks a feather, chirrup, chirrup.
I call her lady, the little finger curls over the teacup.
I call her precious, jewel, her face catches the light.
I call her my doll, she has real hair, her eyes open and shut.
I call her my dove. Wings white against the blue
she wheels, perches, takes grain from my palm.
I call her my own.

The gold ring circles the third finger of her left hand.

She is my better half, my sweetheart, my love, my life.
Her name is Elisabeth. Bess. Bessie. My wife.

To me, Bessie! Bessie, to me! She comes to my call,
she comes cringing, belly upwards. I say, Bess
when I say bye you must go bye, when I say here
you must come here, when I say come away back Bess,
back you must go. That's enough Bess! Stay!

I call her flesh of my flesh. She is tearing
her flesh with her teeth, she tears herself apart.
I call her heart of my heart.
She is eating her heart out now and
does not answer whatever I say.

RUNNING

Sweet gilt gingerbread boy
the one she always wanted
jumps from the oven
done to a turn, she could
eat him up! But the door
isn't a door, it's ajar and he's
running too fast and too soon
past the old bitch, past the cow,
away down the lane
he's the gingerbread man
catch as catch can.

Climb on my tail sharp lad
I'll carry you
over the one-strand river.
Creep up my back
as the water rises
I'll take you
wherever you want to go.
Crawl up my neck, right up
to my black black nose.

Snap! The lad's disarmed.
Snap! The boy's legless.
Snap! goes the gin-toothed trap
he's lost his head.

Running in circles now
he doesn't come home to tea
she opens the oven. Flat
gingerbread boys have black
burnt currant eyes. She nibbles
a leg, an arm, a head.
All gone!

RONDEAU REDOUBLE

There is so little left. The room is bare.
She'll strip his sheets and blankets by and by.
Only this morning he was sleeping there.
The light is pouring from a hard white sky.

She'll write to him, perhaps he will reply?
He's better off she knows, God knows, elsewhere.
She'd be all right, she told him cheerfully.
There is so little left. The room is bare.

His smell's still hanging in the chilly air,
his motor-cycle boots are propped awry,
helmet abandoned in the basket chair.
She'll strip his sheets and blankets by and by.

Make a fresh start. Do something useful. Try
to avoid that stunned and slightly foolish stare
the mirror offers her maternal eye.
Only this morning he was sleeping there.

He's left a paperback face downwards where
he gave up reading and she lets it lie.
That's not his footstep on the wooden stair.
The light is pouring from a hard white sky.

She stacks up papers, pulls the covers high,
faces the glass now, plucks the odd grey hair,
flicks away cobwebs, dusts off a dead fly,
feels and tries not to feel her own despair.
There is so little left.

SOFT FRUIT

Each summer she would fight the difficult
green netting out of the garage and, cursing,
drape swathes on the frame over the bushes
against the blackbirds and invading thrushes.

It almost always rained when the soft fruit
ripened but she'd be out there, picking
an hour or more each afternoon, wet canes
drenching her trousers above the wellies.

Sorting out bad ones, picking out leaves, grubs,
forking off strigs, she'd make pies, creams, sorbets,
tarts and cheesecakes, fruit fool, summer pudding,
calling the children to the sweet red harvest.

End of the season she'd strip the bushes,
cut the canes back ready for next summer.
Her larder is stocked with jams and jellies
but nobody's home these days, much, to eat them.

Now she lies out in the sun all summer
among the bushes, calling the blackbirds,
the spotted thrushes. Feel free, my children,
come, help yourselves. You are welcome. Welcome.

AFTERLIFE

In the heart of the house
in the marriage chamber
laid to rest
the lovely lady
with her gold chains, her gold rings,
charm-bracelets, love-tokens,
so they will know
when the grave is opened
a rich woman
well provided.

Under the hearthstone
in the great kitchen
peace at last
for the house-keeper.
Ranged by her side her pots and puncheons,
knives, crocks, boards, basins,
so they will know
when they come upon her
a rich woman,
deft, skilful.

Up in the nursery
curled in the cradle
a long lie-in
for the nursing mother.
Under her heart the childrens' pictures,
tucked in her shawl the teddy, the rag-doll,
so they will know
who break her slumber
a rich woman
with many treasures.

Under the apple-tree
down by the goat-shed
laid in earth
the earth-mother.
Planted with her, her spade and trowel,

catalogues and seed-packets
so they will know
at the resurrection
a rich woman
with green fingers.

But through the eye of the needle
poor as a churchmouse
plain as a pikestaff
bare as a bodkin
thin as a pin
I go in, I come out.
I go out, I come in.

REGRET

Remind her that she must not feel regret.
Not an emotion one finds useful, yet
something is hurting and would it be worse
to admit that what she's feeling is remorse?

He would say neither of them was at fault
but white and crystalline the lump of salt
who was his wife. She has to undergo
the agenbite of inwit, will she or no.

Bitter the taste he never liked to savour.
The acid drop. Always her favourite flavour.

THINKING OF YOU

It's not his writing on the little card. They would have
taken the order over the phone. Would he like to
make a selection? Did he have any preference? No,
he would leave it to them, whatever seemed suitable.

Under the transparent wrap twisted tight round the neck
with plastic ribbon the mopheads of chrysanthemums
are damp with condensation, the rose-petals veined deep
crimson, the irises stiff and blue and the thin dark
tongues of lilies poke out from their dead white gold flecked
                                                    throats.

It was a kind thought, was it not? I will acknowledge
the applause which seems to be for someone else, perhaps
the one of whom he was thinking? But as I carry
the flowers back underground I am thinking of him.

I PICK UP THE BALL

run on the spot bouncing it in front of me,
toss it high, catch it with one hand,
spin it on the tips of my fingers,
throw it from one hand to the other,
pass it behind my back,
bounce it between my legs, spin and
sling it underhand to my partner who

drops it.

I laugh, pick up the ball, running lightly
in little circles, patting it gently.
Toss it in the air, head it twice, steady it,
let it roll down my spine slowly, slowly,
arch my back, bounce it off my hip,
to calf, to heel, a sharp kick up and
over to my partner who

drops it.

I pick up the ball keep it in the air
feet going all the time throw the ball
catch the ball turn twist spin
catch it again make with the wrist
one hand two hands AND again HUP!
Head nose hip shin knee elbow HUP!
and toss it to my partner who

drops it again.

I hold the ball close to my chest.

Couldn't you keep it up?
Couldn't you keep it going?

It was all right on the ground.

But that's not the game!

Were we playing a game?

OUT OF THE BOX: ONE

In the nursery the little children
abandoned each morning watch
the trains go round and round as
cold light, comfortless,
falls from high windows. You can see
nothing but sky. Hear
the blows of the axe ring out
from the end of the garden.

We have needed something
to make a clean break but
it makes me weep to see
under the dry brown skin
the white leaves fold so neatly
like prayers around the centre.

Blindfold I put out my hands
to take the apple. How is it with you?
she said kindly. I said, Bitter.
It is what you are offered.
If you cannot accept it
then that is bitter.

Walking the seashore on a knife-edge
a black snake around her throat
she turns young men to stones
and children to changelings. Sheep
miscarry, milk sours, cabbages bolt
and frost blights the orchard.
She paddles a leaky sieve over the surf
with a wooden spoon, her cries
wild and sad as a train at nightfall.

Everything must go

The wooden spoon the toy train the knife
the candle the apple the scarf
the onion the black tights the knife
the black book the empty bowl.

OUT OF THE BOX: TWO

I painted black lines round my eyes
and shadowed my cheekbones for
that hollow look. We played liar-dice.
He won so much I had to doubt his word.

I wore my keys on a red string
like a thin line of blood around my throat.
House keys, car keys, box keys. And what
will these skeleton keys unlock?

We got used to having stone heads
and stared across the desert. It was
lovely in certain lights, shifting
grains, cloud shadows, birds of prey.

This old black blunt-featured
terrible blind mask would once
have seemed alien, savage. Now
the distortions are familiar.

I trace the scars of tribal markings,
the inlaid ivory stare, the teeth
filed sharp, the elongated ear-lobes,
the gold bands ringing the neck.

JUMPING OFF

He could never stand the sight of blood.
I learned to keep my skin unblemished
my stomach flat, breasts firm, joints supple.
There would be no blood, I promised. He
himself devised this thick dark hair, these
long legs, these slender ankles hung with
silver bells that sing as my feet shift.
I wear his scarlet robe though red is
not my colour. I paint my nipples, dance myself
into the ground.

From the boat moored below the village
we walked through fields of artichokes
past the greygreen goldflecked channels
to the Basilica and inside
it is the Day of Judgement. Devils
probe and prong, flames leap and lick and we
are among the damned. The Lady holds
her child to her breast; one jewelled tear
falls down her splendid cheek. She knows
how it will end.

I let the blood flow. My stomach swells
my breasts hang veined and heavy, thunder-
thighs spread wide huge and grotesque I grunt
I bear down. There is a lot of blood.

They shouted JUMP JUMP but I could not
jump, for my life I could not but when
fire scorches your back when flames lick the
stairwell when the child must be saved then
you will jump though you break every bone
in your body.

THE RECEPTION

The lady attendant
hangs up my coat alongside
rows of mink
strung up by their tails
as a warning.

Mine's the rabbit.

Her saucer
holds only five pence:
I placate it
with twenty.

Inside
little black frocks
chitter in high-flown voices.

Diving in
going under
out of my depth
there may yet be a transformation

glitter
sequins
the stately
        descent
            of the staircase.

THE BIRD

This time I'll be avoiding that strict rhyme
that slams the door shut every time,
the clenched fist thumping the rhythm out
along the line, beat of a hard heart.
I'll not be counting syllables for fear
something gets out I can't afford to hear.

For years I kept that fierce bird in her cage,
if she got out, I thought, she'd do some damage
with that hooked beak, those claws. Better
I keep her shut up in rhyme and meter.

But she's been poorly these last days, I see
if it goes on like this she'll die on me.
So I undo the door, untie the string,
risk there'll be no homecoming.

Watch her shuffle to the cage door,
  flip
     plunge
         recover
flick a wing-tip, catch the air
  hover
      circle
         strong now
she's fine now, riding a thermal
  spiralling
        away.

THE POTTERY LESSON

Why do you break your pots as soon as you have made them?

Because they are not right
because I don't like them
because they don't satisfy me
because they are not the way I want them to be
because they are all crooked
because I am ashamed of them
because I am ashamed of myself.

Those are good answers
but they are not the answer.
Why do you break your pots as soon as you have made them?

Because I have made them
because they show too much
because they show it too clearly
because I don't want to look
because I don't want anyone else to look
because I recognise them
because they are mine.

Those are good answers
but they are not the answer.
Why do you break your pots as soon as you have made them?

Because when the clay is broken
soaked in water
wedged on the board
and returned to its original state
then it can be used again.

That is a good answer.
Still, it is not the answer.
Why do you break your pots as soon as you have made them?

I can't answer that question.

When you can answer that question
you will no longer be broken.

THE IRON LADY, THE SNOW QUEEN

The whole thoracic region is rigid.
When we palpate the abdomen
below the rib-cage or probe
the interstices we may note
it is impervious and cold to the touch.
No application of local heat
would seem to penetrate.
The eyes are open; we judge
she is aware of what goes on around her
but is unable to respond.
Moving pictures, drought, earthquake or massacre
do not appear to move.
Sexual imagery, however esoteric
has no effect at all.

The hearing is undoubtedly impaired.
It may be that the cardial system, operating
under conditions of abnormal pressure
inhibits awareness of aural stimuli.
The sense of smell is problematic;
we had difficulty devising appropriate tests.
A cut onion stimulated lachrymation.
We cannot judge if the sense of taste is affected,
it seems things may still be bitter to her.
We doubt if she can experience sweetness.

We have no idea what trauma may have initiated
her condition. We do have evidence
that a small sample of cryogenic material
may, in certain circumstances,
penetrate the chest wall, changing
the condition of the cardiac musculature.
There have been cases when a warm saline solution
applied externally has proved efficacious.
We can find no donor (to date) whose tears
are warm enough or sufficiently salt
to produce any measurable effect.
It is possible that she spontaneously rejects

26

emotional material unless very closely related.
It may be that she rejects all emotional material
even including her own.
We do not know
how long she may continue in this condition.
We will not discuss the question of the quality of life;
this would seem to introduce value judgements
with which we could be reluctant to become involved.

We can only state what seems obvious.

She has a very hard heart.

HALLOWE'EN, WALLINGFORD, PA

The first hard frost this morning. Overhead
the geese skein southward threading a pale sky.
Crickets have fallen silent. Scarlet leaves
dropped from the maples lie like pools of blood.

They cast the bones at random to foretell
the future. Soon it will be Fall.
There will be fires. Nights are drawing in.

Chained to the porch's flake-white posts
his old black legs hang upside-down.
His hands are gloves, his pumpkin head
dangles between his ragman's sleeves.

Straw-man, tormented Brother, light-
bearer for the longest night,
keep the dead souls well away,
keep the wilderness away.

Burn this prisoner in his chains
his spirit rising with the flames
spells the sun's warmth back to earth
keeps the heart's heat in the hearth.

We have safe passage, he's beside us
and his burning flesh will guide us.

An age-old ritual for the season,
it goes way back, an invocation
to raise the spirits of the children.

Between the flake-white posts of the porch
the man hangs crucified head downwards.

FOR EDITH N

Now is the time to forgive that fierce mother
whose round spectacles caught the sun at Blackpool,
whose stockings are creased at the ankle, whose face, resentful
is turned towards Dad who must be holding the Brownie.

She is clutching your hand. Your body, poised, extended
on the diagonal draws the eye out of the picture.
Her face is the face of a jailer but you escaped
and ran when you could. It was the chance of a lifetime.

You came back with gifts but knew they were never enough
to make up for what she had lost, what you had taken.
Her lifetime hung like the surplus flesh on her bones
and all her bright things were the colour of ashes.

Her voice was so small by the end that you almost missed it
and got there too late. But you made the arrangements
and on the whole it was done as you would have wanted.
Now she wants nothing. Now you can start to forgive her.

EMILY

Emily presses her hands against the glass
the doves' pink feet picket the terrace.

Emily dear child treasures her lucky charm
within the circle she can do no harm.

Outside the sky is bleak the world is wide
Emily has a secret she stays inside.

Emily shuts her mouth and keeps it shut,
nothing comes in and she does not got out.

The circle is closed up: she likes it so.
Outside the white doves are on sentry-go.

Emily's wilderness secured. Her star
spindles a black hole further and deeper.

FOR ANNEKATE FRIEDLANDER

If I forget thee, oh Jerusalem, may my right hand forget her cunning.

Annekate's spine's so bent she can only see the floor
and her own feet shuffling in front of her.
Doubled up, her bones crumpled
under their own weight, like an old turtle
pushing the walking-frame over the parquet
she finally makes it to the grand piano.

Transfers her weight from the frame, cautiously
leans on the instrument. Shifts, laborious,
knees bent, nose almost touching the keyboard:
is ready. Only the slow movements, she confesses,
it is in the shoulders and I can no longer
practise four hours a day. Nevertheless
there is a repertoire. Molto lento, these days
but sostenuto.
              Always in her mind
sunrise from a flat roof overlooking a garden
where women lay out washing. Strays dogs. Oranges.
Off the Via Dolorosa a sandal maker
would fix them while you waited. From the baker
we bought chollas for the Sabbath, eggs
from a woman who sold bitter herbs
in spring and lilies in their glory.

Sunlight, silence, singing. The stones
still standing one upon the other.
Brilliant passages, golden blessed city,
milk, honey, fig-trees, olives, ailanthus

Annekate knows it in her bones.
She remembers Jerusalem
and the slow movements are still possible.

POEM FOR MIM

Half the world over, under those golden
copper crimson fire-ball trees, Mim
sounds with an open hand
on the pregnant belly of her red clay drum,
a beat like a great heart.

Mim makes whistles in the shape of birds,
turtles, bears, lizards.
Spirits breathe through them,
they speak in several voices, hoot
squeak and twitter. Mim makes shells
that sing like the sea, clay clappers
tick and tock like forest creatures,
crepitate like crickets while
she holds the rhythm on that heartfelt drum.

The bowl I made held thin air
tense in an approximate circle.
I may use it for paperclips,
hairpins, thumbtacks but
I made it empty.

Mim, teach me how to make
a drum like a beating heart,
a whistle like a free bird
and a round glazed bowl
that will hold fresh water.

KINGS WALK GLOUCESTER

The women can only buy what's on offer
and they must make sure they get their money's worth
because it's the only worth they have. So
they scream at the children strapped to their pushchairs
because they have to learn to behave
nicely.

Later the children run screaming on the grass,
fight one another for toy cars, bikes, rubber balls,
as if they knew there was something they were not
being offered. That's quite enough, says Teacher
but she is wrong. It is nothing like
enough.

But they swallow the rewards they know they have
deserved for behaving so nicely and when
they have eaten everything there's still something
missing, they are still hungry but now (they have learned
to behave) when they scream it sounds like
laughing.

THE TANGLES OF NEAERA'S HAIR

Neaera
in her flaming hair
clasps salamanders
triple-toed, only
strong spirits face them out

combs down pale shoulders
amber waterfalls or
on an ebbing tide
emptying the rock-pool, bronze
tendrils wavering
set with pearls

pins her love-locks high
cloud-cover parting
a blue streak. Up there
beyond the cirrus
sickle swifts
continually fly

plaits her hair with serpents
weaves in those dreadlocks all
their lost entangled faces

(keep your eyes closed
climbing up
your fingers crossed)

wild girl her hair
a mess of cirrus
seaweed
flame.

OLD BETTY BONES

                    surviving
sand-scoured, grief-worn,
in deep water fashions
with crooked fingers white
clay knuckle-bones
strange vertebrae
the skeletons of dreams.

What flesh hung from this scaffold?
What ligament from this cusp
raised what unlikely limb?
What punishing shoulder
did this great blade lift up,
what wild uncertain heart
battered this rib-cage, what
hurt mind so scarred this cranial shell?

She sets them bone to his bone
but does not prophesy in case they live.

How many feet would they have?
How many probing fingers?
How many teeth bared in these jaws,
how many dragon wings would beat the sky
how many heads with flames
with lickerish tongues
with eyes like Catherine Wheels
with dreadful tails?

Betty in the basement
lays out these dry bones
breathless
one by one.

LEAVINGS

The attic. Plastic sheep under the radiator.
Somewhere in the room a small blonde child moves cows and
                                                sheep through
a plastic gate to pasture on a new patch of carpet.

On the windowsill an empty can and a rag. A girl
bucket between her knees soaps the long reins of a bridle.
The radio sings love, love, love but her face is shuttered.

First floor back, a bit of lego is jammed under the door.
Blu-tack scars where a racing-car poster has been taken down.
A boy glues the wing of his glider, waits for it to dry.

First floor left, a stain on the carpet. A gear-box has been
dismantled. She disappears on the back of someone's bike,
her hair flying. The exhaust roars going over the bridge.

First floor right, a cardboard box with two leather belts,
a silk tie, a broken-strapped sandal and an odd sock.
Two people under a duvet who still love each other.

In the bathroom a thin sliver of soap in the bathtub.
A woman sits on the floor reading aloud. Three children
wrapped in towels listen, their backs against the radiator.

Downstairs front, a bit of jigsaw has fallen between
the floorboards. Plain blue sky. Children bend over the puzzle.
It is three-quarters done. They don't know one piece is missing.

In the study under the empty shelves a torn dust-jacket.
Scraps of paper in an apple-box. A man punches up
numbers on his calculator, yawns, pushes his chair back.

The kitchen. Two old jam-jars in the top cupboard. People
are sitting round the table. The meal is almost ready,
she will serve it out, they will eat, they will be together.

DORIS' DAUGHTER

                           is not quite all there but
runs through the market in a tearing hurry
to get there, full of terrible rage, pushing her baby
blindly over the road in the teeth of the world.
A pink bundle with a small dark face she
opens her eyes already apprehensive knowing
it will be years before she can run. Doris' daughter
yells abuse at the whole world which is out
to get her, scoops up the baby holding it close
to her chest she streaks through the city
scatheless as one can pass one's finger through
a candle-flame and not feel pain. But cannot run
fast enough for the baby whose pink stretch-suit
is scorched, whose hair frizzled, whose cry frantic.

THE GIFTED CHILD

He keeps it on a chain
in the shed out back. It howls horribly
and naturally the neighbours complain.
What's the point, they say,
keeping a wild thing like that
if you can't let it run free?

It's so often the way,
people get saddled with gifts
they have no use for. He tried
to abandon it on the motorway,
it found its way back. He tried
to starve it but it lives on air.

He keeps the shed door locked now,
swears blind there's nothing inside
but when he stops talking you can hear
the whimper rising and falling and behind
that closed facade you know it's there

and if you were to open the door
even for a second it would
break your heart.

SUPERSTITION

May blossom clotting the hedgerows
smells like a woman's sex; that
may be why our mothers' mothers
were always forbidden
to bring it into the house.
Unmindful we haul in branches
snuffing the rankness.

We have forgotten why our mothers' mothers
would throw salt over their shoulders,
cut the loaf away from the body,
cross fingers, avoid thirteen at table,
step over cracks in the pavement,
never pass on the stairs
or blow out a candle.

We have forgotten why
we should plant potatoes on Good Friday,
make corn-dollies at harvest,
deck the well-head, bless the seed-corn,
let the field lie fallow one year in seven
say grace before meals
and sing to the rising sun.

But I would not bring May into the house
in case there is something
that has not forgotten.

PRIORY WILD MEADOW

Step over the barrier. Priory Wild Meadow
(thanks to the City Council) is preserved today
as part of our National Heritage, mowed
only from September to May.

Lie flat on your back. Straight above, sky
pierced with the top branches of willows,
bound round the edge with buttercup, blackberry,
twitch-grass, plantain, burdock, briar-rose.

Do not turn your head far enough
to see power-lines loop pylon to pylon,
a workshop's low-pitched asbestos roof,
blank-faced warehouses blocking the horizon.

Breathe shallow so as not to admit
the ring-road stink of petrol and melting tar,
the windblown dust of dried dog-shit,
the whiff of brackish river water.

Shut your ears against the implacable
mutter of traffic, the thump of a compressor,
the screaming of metal against metal,
the buzz of light aircraft going over.

Lie in the middle of Priory Wild Meadow
(not more than a few yards across)
eyes fixed, ears shut, not breathing. So
you preserve your inheritance. So what is lost?

MOURNING DARREN

Little cheep-cheepy children
riding the big machines
make a brave show. Give us a go!
He gunned off gleeful towards Gilpin Bridge
and took the corner wrong.

Cheepy-cheep children
wearing pink, white, peppermint green
(black's not in this year
at Pop Shop, Polly Perkins, Jean Machine)
watch Darren's box slide through
and cry like children.

Chicken children
hurl themselves off the edges of their lives
as if they were worth nothing. Look at me!
Watch me! Careful, their mothers warn.

Evening the pool is empty. Blue water
rocks and rocks back to stillness. Black
lines waver along the bottom.
       Black
in respect of fine men greatly missed,
black for beloved grandads, great
aunts and monstrous uncles but for him
white, pink, peppermint green
is the colour of mourning.

END OF PARANOID INCIDENT

Yesterday evening on the box he said
NO WAY, AMANDA! and she understood
that she must change her name.

EVERYTHING MUST GO. She must keep nothing back,
a FINAL CLEARANCE. MONSTER SALE. REDUCTIONS.
Already her monsters are much reduced,
there will be FREE GIFTS perhaps?
She is expecting a FREE OFFER
(subject to availability, while stocks last.)

At the checkout he is holding
a scrap of paper, folded, but she could read
REMEMBER HEART: MILES: WALKING SHOES.

She remembers Miles' heart.
Puts on her walking shoes.

The forecast suggests there will be a deep depression
but it will pass. The South will escape the storm.
Over the air he said; GOODNIGHT MIRANDA. Of course
he would know about the name.
Driving South it is possible
to see the signs: NO MARKINGS FOR MILES.

Now there is HEAVY PLANT CROSSING
crunching the tarmac under metal treads
and a warning: BEAR RIGHT.
She has never found that easy but she follows
the arrows LEFT with their assurance
that the ROAD WORKS.
                    And so reaches THE END.

They apologise for any inconvenience.

MAISEMORE HAM

The Severn runs dead
slow
the colour of sin.

The loose trains of the willows' dropping hair
crimped in black curlpapers mourn
over the dirty cold polluted stream.

Small grubby sheep crop the unwholesome grass.
The Cathedral tower is trapped in scaffolding.
High tension wires sag with the weight of sky.

Wasteground
ringroad
filling station
carwash.
The concrete cracks. Oh see
the sun goes down in an angry sky.

We have gone too far. The heart
is all gone out of things and we must make
our own way home.

THIS GATE MUST BE KEPT SHUT AT ALL TIMES

inside
leaves turn gold   turn red   crisp
and fall

at all times
children flower pale and fragile
trundling their tricyles over the bruised grass

outside
old men on benches smoke   drink cider   piss
in the corners

outside
people leave cars   return   stow packages
drive off   their radios howling.

at all times
gulls mew   bark   jeer from the rooftops
at dusk bells ring down changes

outside
drunken boys chase one another cursing

at all times
this gate must be kept shut

with difficulty   a baulk
jams the two leaves together
a cane wedged through rusty hoops
to stop it blowing open

at all times
inside a wild unsleeping light
on brickwork pediment and glazing turns
the dying trees to stone.

POOR JENNY LIES AWEEPING

Jenny stands in the middle of the room
she is screaming SILENCE! SILENCE!
THE NOISE IS DRIVING ME MAD!
And we are all ashamed
to be driving Jenny mad
and we are silent.
But Jenny can't hear the silence
because she is screaming.

Jenny sits in a darkened room
she is screaming LIGHT! LIGHT!
And we are all standing by the door
holding lighted candles
but Jenny can't see us
because her eyes are closed
because she is afraid of the dark.

Jenny lies beside the river
she is screaming WATER! WATER!
I AM AS DRY AS A BONE!
We are all swimming, we say
Jump in Jenny, the water's lovely!
But Jenny can't move
because she is in such pain.

She only has to stop screaming
to hear the silence.
She only has to open her eyes
to see the candles
floating down river.
She only has to reach out
to touch the water.

THE PICTURE IS BURNE-JONES' *'Green Summer'*,
THE MUSIC IS MOZART

The strings are twisted together holding the girls
in a group on the grass in a green twilight.

Lovely women langorous with green sickness,
their heads too heavy with tresses to hold upright.

I'll tell you a secret! A pale serpent
supports the book for her to read out the passage.

The music darkens. Now the horns and cellos
are telling the girls perhaps they ought not to listen.

The trees suggest nightfall. And out beyond the picture
a clear sky patterned with dipping swallows.

In their green meadow the girls lean closer together.
They can't keep their heads straight or their eyes open.

GLOUCESTER: EASTER

Dead water
lispslopslips
rocks
milkcartons, beercans, lemonade bottles
takeway boxes
reeds
twigs
rope-ends, fag-ends.

A saw screams from across the dockscape,
Up above a small airplane bumbles
rope slaps loose over dead water
lispslipslops expanded polystyrene.

An old man sweeps dust, fag-ends, spent matches,
blown leaves, dust, dust, fag-ends, spent matches.

Gulls yell bark cat-call
take off from the prison roof
and land again baying:

Silence in Priday Metford where
the grinding is ceased.

In the city centre
the daughters of mourning
in their new dresses
wait on cold pavements
for something to open.

WITHOUT

In the corner by the toilets
where you go up to the multistorey
hunched up with her head on her knees
and her plastic bag beside her.

He crouches down, his blue trousers
tight over his knee-caps, his keys
hanging from thick fingers.
Are you all right, Mother?

She is not his mother.

It's amazing, she used to say
when they were small and want
want want you know the way they go?
Want an ice-cream, want a plastic dinosaur,
want a new t-shirt, want a packet of crisps,
want a comic and she couldn't afford
to buy them everything they wanted though
she'd have given them the whole world on a plate
if she could but she used to say
it's amazing what you can do without.

WHO'S AFRAID?

I don't eat meat, I'm afraid.
I don't eat any dairy products,
or sugar, salt, or artificial sweeteners.
It's inconvenient but I'm afraid
I don't eat processed food of any kind
because of the additives. I don't smoke
I don't drink coffee, tea or alcohol,
I drink only purified bottled water.
I don't take drugs, even on prescription.

Stay out of the rain, it is killing the forests.
Stay out of the sun, the ozone layer is thinning.
Stay out of the sea, it is thick with oil and sewage.
Stay out of the air, it is heavy with heavy metals.

Sterilize the drinking vessels
the eating vessels the knives and forks
and all the working surfaces. Everything
must be sterile.

I am no longer sexually active.

Seal the door and windows.
Keep a light burning day and night.

MARCH 15th

Going North a tyre bursts, the car
leaps the central reservation, skids
out of control. I do not intend
to drive up the motorway.

Letters drop innocently through the slot.
Not a final demand, not some obligation
I have overlooked. That small package
does not contain an incendiary device.

On my way to the shops I do not walk
heedless into the path of a bus.
The neighbour's dog does not snap at me,
does not have rabies.

The knife I use for the tomato is not
particularly sharp, it does not slip.
The egg I eat lightly boiled is not
infected with salmonella.

Walking the river path I do not attract
the attention of the tall youths who
push one another, swear, swagger away not
leaving me stunned, bleeding.

I pick my way along the railway line
avoiding the rusty nail which does not
penetrate the sole of my shoe to pierce
the skin. I do not catch tetanus.

At supper I do not choke on a fishbone.
My banana-skin does not fall on the floor,
I do not slip on it, I do not break my hip.

I am not so unwise as to take the electric fire
into the bathroom and balance it
on the edge of the bath.

Lying in the warm soapy water I do not
slit my wrists.

I take only one sleeping pill.

DELAWARE COUNTY, PA

The funeral director has the biggest house.
At every intersection there is a bank,
a hamburger place, a pizza palace,
a do-nut shop, a real-estate office,
a motel and a filling station but
the funeral director's house
is biggest.

A flight of stairs upholstered
in bright green plastic grass
lead to the front door where
four fluted pillars hold up
a classical pediment. Four
white framed windows flank the door
Old Glory flaunts itself
over the close-cut lawn.

The bank is bright, the drugstore
blazes with tinsel, the Ford concession
flutters with glitter-strip
the orthodontist has a big sign,
the pediatrician and the attorney
are uninhibited, the do-nut shop
flickers all night long,
neon arrows beckon to the Fried Chicken,
coloured lights decorate the ice-cream parlour,
the bank has a drive-in cash dispenser
but the House of Death
is biggest.

The dead are rich.
They lie down to rest
in mahogany boxes closed
with intricate brass clasps,
kept at controlled temperatures
and wreathed about with fresh flowers.
They are sung to sleep
with soft music.

DOROTHY NIMMO was born in Manchester, educated in York and Cambridge and worked as an actress in London. She spent the 1960s in Geneva but came back to England in 1970 to Peterborough where she brought up four children, gardened and kept goats.

After her divorce in 1980 she moved to Lancaster where she joined her first creative writing course. In 1989 she took an MA in Creative Writing at Lancaster University and then spent nine months at Pendle Hill, a Quaker Centre for Study and Contemplation in Pennsylvania. She returned to live in Gloucester where she is caretaker of the Friends Meeting House and cook at a vegetarian restaurant.

Dorothy Nimmo's poems and short stories have been published in a variety of magazines and anthologies. She has won prizes at the Cardiff, Bridport, South Manchester and Prema competitions.